FESTIVAL FUN
for the Early Years

RAMADAN
and
EID-UL-FITR

- Fun activity ideas •
- Photocopiable resources •
- Information on customs and beliefs •

SCHOLASTIC

Carole Court

CREDITS

COLEG SIR GAR

Dawson   13-10-06

15 - 00

372.
840
COU

Author
Carole Court

Editor
Victoria Lee

Assistant Editor
Jennifer Shiels

Series Designer
Catherine Mason

Cover Illustration
Catherine Mason

Illustrations
Bethan Matthews

Text © 2005
© 2005 Scholastic Ltd

Published by Scholastic Ltd
Villiers House
Clarendon Avenue
Leamington Spa
Warwickshire
CV32 5PR

www.scholastic.co.uk

Printed by Bell & Bain

1 2 3 4 5 6 7 8 9   5 6 7 8 9 0 1 2 3 4

British Library Cataloguing-in-Publication Data
A catalogue record for this book is available from the British Library.

ISBN 0-439-96491-1
ISBN 9780439964913

Acknowledgement
Qualifications and Curriculum Authority for the use of extracts from the QCA/DfEE document *Curriculum Guidance for the Foundation Stage* © 2000 Qualifications and Curriculum Authority.

Barbara Moore for the use of *King Hakim's garden, Mohammed and the old lady, Ramadan is over!, Eid is here!, Eid night, Let's celebrate* © 2005, Barbara Moore (previously unpublished)

CONTENTS

INTRODUCTION

Celebrating festivals with young children

Young children find it easier to take in new information about a festival if they can relate it to their own experiences. When discussing Ramadan or Eid-ul-Fitr, you could talk about buying new clothes for special occasions, eating party food or attending a place of worship. Do not assume that children can tell you about their celebrations, but families may be willing to give you more details based on their own experiences.

Present the information in a way that the children can understand by telling it in the form of a story. If you do not have any children who celebrate the festival in your group, you could hold up two pictures of a girl and a boy cut from magazines. Give the children names and say that they are, for example, Muslim. Describe some everyday details about each child, such as the patterns on their socks and their favourite toys, then go on to describe how they prepare for the festival and celebrate it. Invite the children to add their own comments and experiences that they have in common with the two children. When you tell any festival story, explain that the girl and boy listened to this story, too.

Multicultural awareness

Give the children first-hand experiences of the items and customs of the festival that you are celebrating, by setting up your home corner to represent a decorated home. Ask parents, community members or religious centres to lend you items. If possible, arrange for groups of children to go shopping for relevant items from local shops, or buy them from educational suppliers (see 'Resources' on page 48). Occasionally eat 'festival' food, not only at the time of the festival but also at other times of the year.

Involving parents and the community

If possible, ask families to send in photographs or short home videos of their festival celebrations. Invite parents into your setting to talk about how they celebrate festivals in their homes and to demonstrate some typical festival cookery ideas. Encourage grandparents to visit too, explaining how the celebration of the festival may have changed over time, or comparing celebrations in other countries. If possible, arrange a visit to a nearby place of worship, such as a Mosque.

How to use this book

This book covers the festivals of Ramadan and Eid-ul-Fitr. For each festival, there is a section of background information and a full-colour poster with suggestions for its use. There is a story associated with each festival, as well as six pages of cross-curricular ideas, plus rhymes and photocopiable activities. The 'Festival planner' topic web shows how the cross-curricular ideas link to the six Areas of Learning. In addition, for each festival, there are six further ideas focusing on craft and gift ideas, cookery, display, role-play, drama and 'Hold your own celebration'.

Dates

● Ramadan is the ninth month of the Muslim year. This period of fasting and spirituality lasts for the entire month.

● The Muslim year is a lunar calendar with months consisting of 29–30 days. This results in the Muslim year being ten or 11 days shorter than the Gregorian one in general Western use, and Ramadan appears to 'move' each year. There are 354 days in the Muslim year.

● As with all lunar calendars, predicting future dates can only be approximate. It is advisable, therefore, to contact the local community to confirm the exact date each year.

● The Muslim calendar (Hijrah) was adopted soon after the death of the Prophet Mohammed. It is thought that the lunar calendar was probably used because, in desert areas, the phases of the moon are a clear way to measure time.

Religious beliefs

● Ramadan marks the time when the Prophet Mohammed began to receive messages from Allah through the angel Jibril (Gabriel). The Qur'an was eventually written down after his death.

● Allah is the Muslim word for 'God'. The Qur'an reveals 99 names for God. These are attributes of God, such as Al-Basir (The All-Seeing) and Al-Hadi (The Guide).

● The Prophet Mohammed set out rules for living the Muslim way. Five of the most important rules are known as the 'Pillars of Islam':

Shahadah – belief in God, a declaration of faith

Salah – regular prayer, five times a day

Zakah – giving to charity

Sawm – fasting during Ramadan

Hajj – visiting the city of Makkah at least once in a lifetime (Makkah is the birthplace of the Prophet Mohammed).

● Fasting during Ramadan is a sign of complete submission to Allah, who is more important than food and drink. Rich and poor are seen as equal since they all share similar experiences.

● Islam has fasting in common with most of the other major religions, including Christianity, Hinduism and Judaism.

Customs and traditions

● Muslims aim to live by common rules, as established by the Prophet Mohammed.

● The Qur'an has been translated into a number of languages, but many Muslims still take pride in being able to recite it in Arabic.

● Around the world there are local variations in custom. Types of food and clothes can vary between different Muslim communities.

● Owing to certain customs and traditions, some children may be reluctant to take part in anything involving music and singing, have photographs taken or eat sweets containing gelatin. It is important to talk to families about their own traditions and not to make assumptions and generalisations.

RAMADAN
BACKGROUND INFORMATION AND PLANNING

Celebrations
● The tradition of fasting goes back to the time of the Prophet Mohammed and is one of the Five Pillars of Islam.
● Muslims fast during the hours of daylight unless they are too ill, too old, too young or travelling. Any day missed can be made up later or additional money can be given to the poor.
● Ramadan is a time for spiritual cleansing when people try to live their lives free from greed, selfishness, envy or lies. It is a time to think about what it is like to be poor, and this is a great leveller. There is a community spirit with a shared sense of purpose through a difficult time.
● During the last ten days many people spend more time at the Mosque and might wait there all night when it is time for the celebration of Eid to start. When the crescent moon is seen, indicating the new month, Ramadan ends.
● For Muslims, the moon is a universal symbol that can be seen and shared by all – wherever they are and whatever language they speak.

Things to remember
● Friday is the day to visit the Mosque for prayer and teaching.
● When acting stories, the character of the Prophet Mohammed should not be portrayed.
● Muslim families do not generally eat pork or other derivatives of pig.
● There are two main festivals: Eid-ul-Adha (which ends the period of Hajj when Muslims try to visit the holy city of Makkah) and Eid-ul-Fitr (at the end of Ramadan – 'Eid' meaning happiness and festivity in Arabic, and 'Fitr' meaning breaking fasts). This book concentrates on Eid-ul-Fitr.
● As a general rule, it is advisable to avoid the use of human and animal illustrations in relation to Islam. They can be seen as offensive to some Muslims.

Using the poster
● Muslims pray to Allah five times a day at set times:
　Fajr – dawn to sunrise
　Zuhr – midday to mid afternoon
　Asr – mid to late afternoon
　Maghrib – after sunset
　Isha – after twilight.
● If it is not possible to go to the Mosque, Muslims find a clean, quiet place to pray and use a prayer mat. They turn towards the Ka'ba at the centre of the Grand Mosque in Makkah. This is believed to be the site of the House of God originally built by Abraham. Before praying, Muslims perform wudu – the washing ritual of hands, face and feet. Shoes are removed before the special sequence of prayers takes place. There are specific steps to the prayer, which are repeated a different number of times depending on the time of day. Prayers can be to praise Allah or to ask for guidance. Personal prayers might also be said.

FESTIVAL FUN
for the Early Years

RAMADAN and **EID**

RAMADAN
FESTIVAL PLANNER

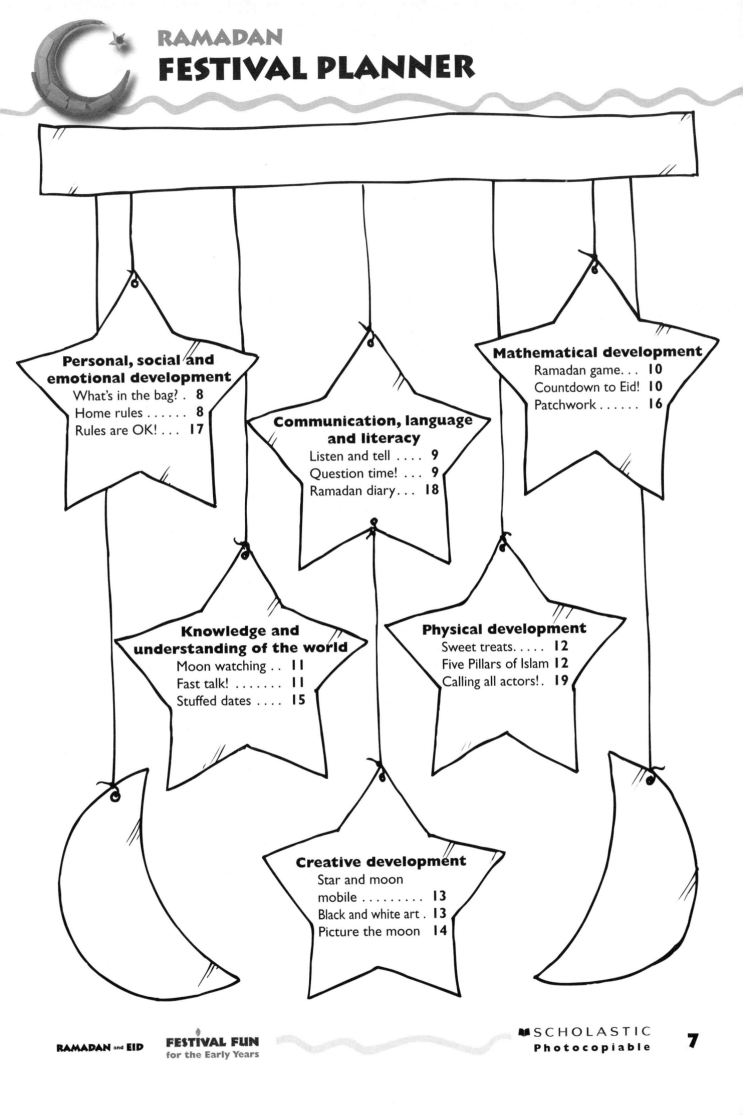

CROSS-CURRICULAR IDEAS

Personal, social and emotional development

RAMADAN

WHAT'S IN THE BAG?

Early Learning Goal
Have a developing respect for their own cultures and beliefs and those of other people.

Talk About
Discuss the need to treat religious objects with respect. Talk about how the artefacts are used, for example, prayer beads remind worshippers of how many times they have repeated a prayer, and the prayer mat provides a clean space to pray.

What you need
The Qur'an; large feely bag; selection of artefacts (for example, prayer beads and prayer hat – see 'Resources' on page 48); table or high shelf; hand-washing facilities.

What to do
● Show the Qur'an to the children. Explain that it is a very special book to Muslims and you are going to treat it with the utmost respect. Place the book on a table or high shelf.
● Show the children the selection of artefacts. Ask them to wash their hands before touching them.
● Remind the children that these artefacts have religious significance and should be treated with respect. Then, let the children carefully handle them.
● Explain their use and encourage the children to talk about the different artefacts.
● Choose a child and, without that child seeing, place an artefact into the large feely bag. Ask the child to guess which object it is. The child can feel the bag and ask other children questions. Repeat with other children and artefacts.

HOME RULES

Early Learning Goal
Understand what is right, what is wrong, and why.

Talk About
Discuss how the family benefits from having rules. Rules are present in all parts of our lives. Within Islam there are rules for the way in which people should live (for example, not to lie or steal). Fasting during Ramadan is one of those rules.

Further Ideas
● Discuss giving to charity – one of the rules or Pillars of Islam.
● Fasting is one of the 'rules' of Islam. Talk about the other rules for Muslim adults (see 'Religious beliefs' on page 5).

What you need
Display board; dark backing paper; large paper stars (yellow, if possible); writing materials; glue.

Preparation
Cover the display board with dark backing paper.

What to do
● This activity can be linked to the 'Rules are OK!' activity on page 17. Discuss the rules that children are aware of in their daily lives, for example, not walking in front of cars. Why are there rules?
● Talk about the rules that they have at home. Discuss what happens when the rules are broken.
● Give out a few stars each. Encourage the children to write or draw on them some of these rules. (Be sensitive to individual home circumstances.) Assist children who are inexperienced writers.
● Arrange and glue the stars on to the board so that they are in clusters according to the rule. Which rule is mentioned most?

**Communication, language
and literacy**

LISTEN AND TELL

What you need

No more than 12 children; 'King Hakim's garden' photocopiable sheet on page 20; 'Story cards' photocopiable sheet on page 23; thin card; scissors.

Preparation

Practise the story so that it can be told rather than read. Photocopy the story cards on to thin card, cut out and laminate if possible.

What to do

● Explain that Muslim children might hear this story during Ramadan and you would like the group to listen carefully so that they can retell it later.
● Tell the story and use your voice to add interest.
● Distribute the story cards between pairs of children. Ask them to discuss the content and decide which part of the story it illustrates. They can then report back to the whole group.
● Retell the story with the children adding the illustrations at the appropriate times.
● Start a 'circle story'. Ask individual children to listen carefully to each contribution and then add the next part of the story.

Early Learning Goal Retell narratives in the correct sequence, drawing on language patterns of stories.

Talk About Tell the children that stories of the Prophet Mohammed are also remembered during Ramadan. It would not, however, be appropriate to act his part in a play.

QUESTION TIME!

What you need

Visitor to answer questions (either a Muslim child or an adult willing to act the role).

What to do

● Before the visit, inform the children that they will be having a special visitor to answer questions about Ramadan.
● Rehearse possible questions, for example, 'What do you do when you go to the Mosque?' and so on.
● On the day of the visit, ask the children to help to prepare for the guest. Remind them of the way to behave with visitors – especially saying 'please' and 'thank you'. Ask one child to welcome the visitor.

● Invite the children to question the guest. Add supplementary questions if necessary.
● On a separate occasion, send a 'thank you' card to the visitor.

Early Learning Goal Speak clearly and audibly with confidence and control and show awareness of the listener, for example by their use of conventions such as greetings, 'please' and 'thank you'.

Talk About Encourage questions about all aspects of Ramadan. It is seen as a duty among Muslims and affects their whole life.

Further Ideas
● Read to the children the rhyme 'Mohammed and the old lady' on page 21. Stop after the third verse and ask the children to predict the ending.
● Use a tape recorder to record the children's own experiences of waiting for an event or festival. Were the feelings of anticipation similar to those felt towards the end of Ramadan?

Mathematical development

RAMADAN GAME

Early Learning Goal

In practical activities and discussion begin to use the vocabulary involved in adding and subtracting.

Talk About

During Ramadan, Muslims try to turn away from selfishness, laziness, greed and anger. They learn to be more kind, considerate and thankful for what they have.

What you need
Copies of 'Gameboard' photocopiable sheet (enlarged) and 'Game dice' photocopiable sheet on pages 24 and 25 for each child; colouring and drawing materials; child scissors; glue; counters.

What to do
● Talk to the children about how they can become more considerate. Ask the children to illustrate these suggestions around the track on the gameboard.
● Invite the children to cut out their dice from the 'Game dice' photocopiable sheet (adult support may be required). Explain that the numerals are in English and Arabic. Arabic is the language used by Muslims all over the world.
● Help the children to fold the dice and glue it together carefully.
● Divide the children into groups to play the game, taking turns to throw the dice and move the counters the correct number of places. Use mathematical vocabulary, for example, 'more', 'plus', 'add', 'addition' and 'forward'. The first one to reach the Eid party wins.

COUNTDOWN TO EID!

Early Learning Goal

Say and use number names in order in familiar contexts.

Talk About

Show the children examples of Islamic patterns. Discuss the shapes and colours used. Many will be geometrical and symmetrical.

Further Ideas

● Read the rhyme 'Ramadan is over!' on page 22 to the children, concentrating on the numbers at the beginning of each verse.
● Make a paper chain with a chain for every day of Ramadan. Remove one chain each day.

What you need
Large piece of card; large numerals written on the centre of pieces of card – one for each day of Ramadan; blue and yellow colouring materials; long strip of green paper; glitter; glue.

What to do
● Write 'Countdown to Eid' on the large piece of card.
● Explain that you would like to make a calendar to count down the days to Eid.
● Use the numbered cards to practise counting forwards and backwards.
● Ask the children to decorate the numerals using the colours blue and yellow, which are popular in Islamic art. Remind them that they should not use people or animals in their work.
● Let some of the children decorate the 'Countdown to Eid' card and use glitter to make it special. Attach this to the top of the green paper strip.
● Work with the children to order and fix the decorated numerals to the strip.
● During Ramadan, remove a number each day in the countdown to Eid.

RAMADAN
CROSS-CURRICULAR IDEAS

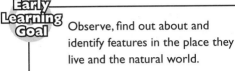

Knowledge and
understanding of the world

MOON WATCHING

Early Learning Goal
Observe, find out about and identify features in the place they live and the natural world.

Talk About
During Ramadan, Muslims observe the moon and wait for the first viewing of the new moon. They then know that the month of Ramadan is over and they can begin their Eid celebrations.

What you need
Letters to families; paper to send home; long strips of paper for each child; glue; display area.

What to do
● Before Ramadan begins, write to families and ask adults to work with the children to observe the moon weekly and keep a record.
● Explain that you would like families to observe the shape and

position of the moon, and draw this on the paper provided. (If the moon is not visible by bedtime, the adults can make the observation and discuss this with the child.)
● Keep your own record for children whose families are not taking part. Prepare a display area and use it to record progress. When the drawings are brought in, ask the children to stick them on to their strip of paper. Talk about the changes that the children observe.

FAST TALK!

Early Learning Goal
Begin to know about their own cultures and beliefs and those of other people.

Talk About
Islam is not the only religion that includes fasting – Judaism, Hinduism and Christianity also encourage it. Explain that Muslim children usually start to fast for Ramadan at about age 12, although many will have fasted for short periods beforehand.

Further Ideas
● Organise a visit to a Mosque.
● Use reference books to find out about the moon and list any facts the children discover.
● Make a book about Ramadan.

What you need
Circle-time object, such as a soft toy; large circle of paper to represent a plate; drawing and writing materials.

What to do
● Ask the children to sit in a circle to discuss healthy lifestyles, especially eating, drinking and sleeping. Pass the object around the group and invite each child to contribute. Talk about the requirements for growth and energy, and the need for water.
● Introduce the paper circle and ask the children to take turns to draw or write their suggestions about a healthy lifestyle on it.
● Explain the difference for adults who are no longer growing taller. Can their bodies cope with fasting? Do the children think it would be a good idea for children to fast?
● Discuss the benefits that fasting for religious purposes may bring, for example, helps people to understand the needs of the poor, gives an opportunity to share a difficult challenge, provides a chance to thank God for good things and so on.

CROSS-CURRICULAR IDEAS

Physical development

SWEET TREATS

What you need
Dates or apricots soaked in syrup; 'Eid is here!' photocopiable sheet on page 42; small pieces of fruit to eat.

Preparation
Check with parents or carers for any allergies or dietary requirements first.

What to do
● Sit the children in a small discussion group. Read the first half of the story that tells of the family fasting and how they break their fast ready for Eid.
● Talk about why adult Muslims fast during Ramadan and explain that many children look forward to the time when they can do the same.
● Discuss how you would feel after a day of fasting. What could make you feel physically better quickly?
● Show the children the dates or apricots soaked in syrup and explain that most Muslims break their fasts by eating something sweet.
● Ask the children to think of reasons why most Muslim children do not fast. Would it be good for growing children to go without food and water?
● Offer each child a piece of fruit to enjoy.

Early Learning Goal Recognise the importance of keeping healthy and those things which contribute to this.

Talk About Muslims fast to remind themselves of less fortunate people who have little or no food. They also give financially to the poor and needy. Explain that the fasting is from sunrise to sunset, so the length of time varies according to the time of year and location.

FIVE PILLARS OF ISLAM

What you need
Pictures of pillars, especially those used in Islamic architecture; range of construction materials, for example, construction kits, bricks, rolled newspapers, Plasticine and recycled materials; display area covered with a green cloth; card for labels; pen; child scissors; glue; sticky tape.

What to do
● Show the pictures of pillars and discuss their use and shape. Point out their great strength and support.
● Ask the children to work in pairs to make their own pillars using the construction materials. Some children may need support to cut materials. Encourage them to consider ways to improve their models.
● Label the models and carefully place them in the display area. Talk to the pairs of children about the construction process.

Early Learning Goal Handle tools, objects, construction and malleable materials safely and with increasing control.

Talk About Explain that there are five Pillars of Islam (see 'Religious beliefs' on page 5). These are the duties that all adult Muslims try to perform. Remind the children that, just as physical pillars support structural buildings, the five Pillars are rules that support Muslims.

Further Ideas
● Thread moon and star shapes together to make a paper chain.
● Taste food from a range of predominantly Muslim countries (remember to check first with parents for allergies and dietary requirements).

CROSS-CURRICULAR IDEAS

Creative development

STAR AND MOON MOBILE

Early Learning Goal Explore colour, texture, shape, form and space in two or three dimensions.

Talk About Discuss the significance of the moon. Muslims watch for the new moon to signify the end of Ramadan and the beginning of Eid. Stars can be seen along with the moon in the night sky. Explain that these symbols can usually be found on Mosques.

What you need
Hoop; string; pre-cut card stars and moons; glue; hole punch; thin thread; wide variety of yellow and gold collage materials with varied textures, for example, foil, fabric, feathers, sand, tissue paper, wool, tissue balls and paint.

What to do
● Give each child a pre-cut star or moon. Explain that you would like them to cover both sides of their shape with the collage materials provided.
● When completely dry, find the point of balance near the edge of each shape and make a hole in it, and attach the thread.
● Tie all the shapes to the hoop, varying the lengths of the thread.
● Work with the children to make it balance. Observe how the weight and length make a difference.
● With the string, suspend the hoop in an appropriate place.

BLACK AND WHITE ART

Early Learning Goal Use their imagination in art and design, music, dance, imaginative and role play and stories.

Talk About Discuss the importance of the Qur'an to Muslims. Explain that it is their Holy Book. It says that, during Ramadan, Muslims can eat and drink at night 'until you can plainly distinguish a white thread from a black thread'. This black and white 'test' is used to determine the hours of fasting.

What you need
Torch; black and white paper; paint; wax crayons; child scissors; glue; sponges; wool; string; cotton cloth; elastic bands.

What to do
● Encourage the children to create pieces of black and white artwork using a wide variety of materials and techniques, for example, string painting, tie-dying, rubbings, printing, paper weaving and paper cutting.
● Using a torch, take the children in small groups into a darkened room with their work. Can they see the black and white?
● Explain that you are going to turn off the torch for a short time. Do they think they will still be able to distinguish black from white?
● Display the work together with an explanation (see 'Talk About' section).

Further Ideas
● Print a variety of designs using the star and moon as the basic shape.
● Give each child a copy of the 'Ramadan is over!' photocopiable sheet on page 22 and invite them to colour in the illustrations.
● Set up role-play situations in which the fasting at Ramadan plays a part, for example, a character is offered food but refuses and explains why.

Creative development

PICTURE THE MOON

Early Learning Goal

Use their imagination in art and design, music, dance, imaginative and role play and stories.

Group Size

All the children, participating in small groups.

What you need

Paper plates; child scissors; yellow paint; dark and white paper; thin ribbon; printing sponges and vegetables; sharp knife (adult use only); yellow wax crayons; yellow and black powder-paint; paintbrushes; water; flour; glitter; clear glue; salt; squeezy bottles; hole punch; aprons; teaspoon; cup; small mixing bowls.

Preparation

Cut the centre from the plates to provide a circular frame. Make two holes at the top. Cut the paper slightly larger than the removed circle, and the sponges and vegetables into moon shapes. To prepare the squeezy-bottle paint, use equal amounts of flour and salt, and form a squeezable texture by adding paint. Set up the areas to be used and ensure the children are wearing protective clothing.

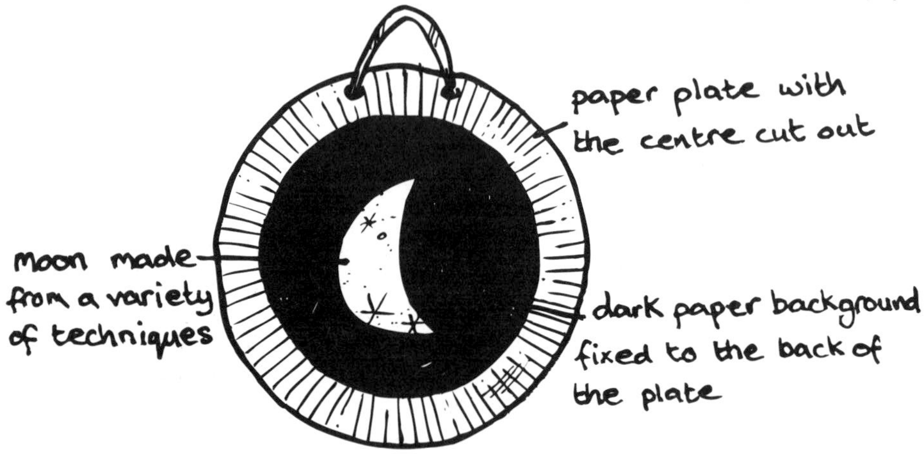
paper plate with the centre cut out
moon made from a variety of techniques
dark paper background fixed to the back of the plate

What to do

- Tell the children that they will be making a Ramadan present for a friend. The moon is particularly relevant at this time of year, so you would like them to make a 'moon picture'.
- Demonstrate different ways to make moon pictures, then support the children in choosing a method:

Sponge and vegetable printing
Dip the shapes into yellow paint and print on to the dark paper.

Crayon etching
Use a yellow wax crayon to draw a moon on to white paper. Colour it very thickly with no white showing. Cover the paper with thin black powder-paint. The paint should resist the wax to reveal a night sky.

Glitter paint
Thicken yellow paint with flour and add glitter. Paint the moon on to dark paper.

Squeezy-bottle painting
Squeeze the yellow paint on to dark paper in the shape of a large moon. Add stars to the night sky.

Salt pictures
Mix together half a cup of salt with a teaspoon of yellow paint powder. Make the shape of the moon on the paper with clear glue. Sprinkle the salt mixture over the moon shape and shake off the loose salt.

- When dry, fix the pictures to the back of the paper-plate frame. Thread the ribbon through the holes and tie with a secure knot.

Support and Extension

Support the less experienced children with the skills needed to form the shapes and apply paint. Give older children more opportunity to experiment and express their own ideas, but staying within the same theme.

Further Ideas

- Create a paper-collage moon picture on separate thick paper and cut it out. Attach it to backing paper with small rings of sticky tape, so that it stands out to create a 3-D effect.
- Make invisible paint by mixing four tablespoons of bicarbonate of soda with four tablespoons of water. Give the children cotton buds to paint a crescent moon, filling it its centre with the mixture. When completely dry, cover with thin watercolour paint to reveal the new moon in the sky.

COOKERY IDEAS

Knowledge and understanding of the world

Early Learning Goal
Begin to know about their own cultures and beliefs and those of other people.

Group Size
Six children, working in pairs.

Support and Extension
Confident writers can try to write the instructions for making stuffed dates by themselves on their own separate paper. Encourage all the children to take part when discussing the stuffed dates recipe and other special foods.

Further Ideas
● Make other sweets by mixing together 200g icing sugar and five tablespoons of condensed milk. Add a little food flavouring and colouring. Shape into small balls or flatten and cut into moon shapes. Decorate with chocolate or small sweets.
● Create decorative boxes for the dates to make into gifts (see 'Box of delights' activity on page 36).
● Give the children opportunities to follow and write up other recipes. Use examples from traditionally Muslim countries.

STUFFED DATES

What you need

For every 12 large stuffed, dates you will need: 50g sultanas, 25g ground almonds, 2 dessertspoons honey (runny), few drops of rose-water; large mixing bowl; mixing spoon; three teaspoons; three small mixing bowls; serving plate; table covering; cookery aprons; scales; sharp knife (adult use only); large piece of paper; writing and drawing materials; washing-up area; hand-washing facilities.

Preparation

Cover the cooking area and make cuts in the dates. Check with parents or carers for any allergies or dietary requirements first.

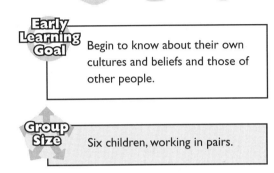

What to do

● Explain to the group that Muslims break their fast with something sweet, such as stuffed dates. Dates are often eaten because the Prophet Mohammed is believed to have broken his fast with them. Traditions vary, but usually a sweet dish and a drink of water are followed by 'iftar' – the evening meal. Ask the children to wash their hands and put on cookery aprons.
● Divide the dates between the pairs of children and ask them to remove the stones. Work with them to weigh out the sultanas and ground almonds, and pour them into the large mixing bowl.
● Let the children take turns to mix the dry ingredients together.
● Ask one pair to add the honey and rose water. Mix together and observe the changes when wet ingredients are added.
● Divide the mixture in three and share between the pairs of children. Encourage them to continue stirring the mixture thoroughly in their small mixing bowls.
● Ask the children to fill the dates carefully and arrange them on the serving dish.
● Encourage the children to assist in tidying and washing up.
● Invite the children to recount how they prepared the dates. Help them to record each instruction on a large piece of paper for display.
● Ask the children to think of different recipes or foods that are used in other religious festivals or special occasions, for example, Christmas pudding, traditional Indian sweets at Divali and birthday cakes.
● Let the children take the recipe for stuffed dates home to share with family and friends.

Mathematical development

PATCHWORK

Early Learning Goal
Talk about, recognise and recreate simple patterns.

Group Size
Small groups.

What you need
Samples of Islamic art patterns; paper cut into regular hexagons (different colours if possible); large number of pre-cut shapes, including stars and moons, and ensure that there are at least six of each; glue; colouring materials; thick, bright felt-tipped pen; backing paper.

Preparation
Cover the display area with backing paper, and cut the hexagons and star and moon shapes if these are not commercially produced. Collect together examples of Islamic art patterns.

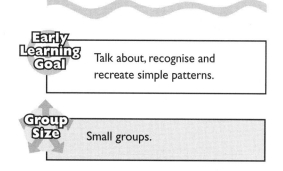

What to do
- Explain that you would like the group to prepare a display that links Ramadan with the festival of Eid. It will incorporate the kind of decoration to be used during Eid.
  - Tell the children that they will be making a patchwork display from hexagons. Ask them what they notice about this shape – how many sides does it have? Is each side equal in size?
  - Talk to the children about the ways in which Muslims use Ramadan as a time of reflection and thought.
  - Ask the children to suggest ways in which they can be more considerate either in the setting or at home.
- Record these on the hexagons in bold print. The children can then add their own ideas by writing or drawing by themselves.
- Show the children the examples of Islamic patterns. Point out the use of shape, pattern and symmetry. Animals and people will not be found, because the Prophet Mohammed felt that there was a danger of people being tempted to worship them. Green is often used as it was thought to be the Prophet Mohammed's favourite colour.
- Give each child a hexagon and help them to fold it into six equal parts.
- Let the children have a variety of shapes and ask them to decorate their own hexagons in the style of Islamic patterns. Point out the importance of symmetry.
- Demonstrate ways to decorate the edges and creases, and where the shapes can be placed (see illustration).
- Mount the hexagons to form a patchwork of promises and patterns. Add a border and title. Involve the children in arranging the display.

Support and Extension
Assist younger children with the folding of the hexagons. Encourage older children to write their own suggestions and be more creative in their use of patterns.

Further Ideas
- Make a large picture of a prayer mat with the children contributing to the patterns.
- Prepare a display based on the phases of the moon (see 'Moon watching!' on page 11 for ideas). Discuss the moon's significance to Muslims during Ramadan.

Personal, social and emotional development

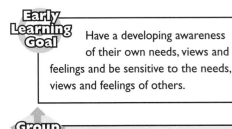

Early Learning Goal
Have a developing awareness of their own needs, views and feelings and be sensitive to the needs, views and feelings of others.

Group Size
Small groups.

RULES ARE OK!

What you need
Large sheet of paper; writing and drawing materials; small pieces of card; Blu-Tack.

Preparation
Arrange for adult support for the role play, if necessary. This activity can be linked to 'Home rules' on page 8.

What to do
● Explain that fasting during Ramadan is one of the 'rules' of Islam. Adult Muslims try to keep to this rule unless they are sick, elderly

or travelling. Ramadan is a time for Muslims to think about how they live their lives and their relationship with others.
● Ask the children if there is any behaviour that makes them unhappy. How do they feel if someone is reluctant to share or leaves an area untidy? Explain that they should not refer to specific individuals from the group.
● Talk about how it feels to be the victim of unkindness. Do they think the person being unkind is happy?
● Consider 'rules' for the role-play area and help the children to compile a list. Emphasise good behaviour, rather than using the word 'don't'. Include such rules as:
– put everything back in its place
– be willing to share
– play together
– be kind to each other
– take turns.
● Use the large sheet of paper to make a poster incorporating all of the rules. Write or illustrate each rule on a separate piece of card.
● Play a game to enable the children to become familiar with the rules. Ask pairs of children to pick a card and then act out their rule (you may need to pair a child with an adult for extra support). Invite the other children to guess the rule. When they have finished, attach the card to the poster with Blu-Tack.
● Display the poster within the role-play area. Refer to it at various times and remind the children about positive behaviour.

Support and Extension
If necessary, arrange for adults to act out the rules for the children to guess. Be prepared to follow up conversations with individual children if they wish to discuss anything further. Ask the children to write their own list of ways to behave.

Further Ideas
● Follow up the children's ideas of how to improve behaviour.
● Extend the rules to behaviour within the whole area.
● Copy the poster and send it home. Encourage families to take part and follow similar rules at home.
● Return to the list at regular intervals. Do the children still feel that they are relevant? Do they feel that the group is managing to keep the rules?

Communication, language and literacy

RAMADAN DIARY

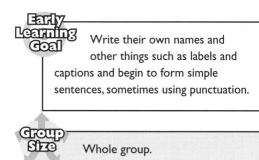

Early Learning Goal
Write their own names and other things such as labels and captions and begin to form simple sentences, sometimes using punctuation.

Group Size
Whole group.

What you need
Copy of 'My Ramadan diary' photocopiable sheet on page 26 for each child and one enlarged copy; child scissors; stapler (adult use only); A4 paper; writing materials.

Preparation
Prepare an enlarged version of the diary for demonstration purposes, by cutting up the sections and stapling them together to make a booklet. Create behaviour tickets by dividing an A4 sheet into 16 sections and drawing a large ✓ on each section. Copy this sheet and cut them up. Distribute the tickets to any other adults present and explain their use.

What to do
● Explain that Ramadan is a serious time for Muslims. It is a time when they consider their lives and the impact of their actions on others.
● Ask the children to think about their actions. How do other people feel when they are kind and unkind?
● Make a list of the children's suggestions for positive behaviour. Include any ideas for being kind and thoughtful.
● Introduce the behaviour tickets. Explain that for the next hour (or any suitable period of time) you, and any other adults present, will be looking out for kind actions. Every time a child is 'caught', they will be given a ticket.
● If possible, a reward could be given to the child with the most tickets.
● Talk about keeping a record of kind behaviour. Explain the idea of keeping a diary and writing something every day.
● Demonstrate how to make the diary and assist the children as they put together their own. Alternatively, you may prefer to make up the diaries beforehand, ready for the children to use.
● Ensure that the children have the title on the front and encourage them to write their names in the correct space.
● Ask the children to take their diaries home to complete them. For each day they should write about their good behaviour, by writing words, simple sentences or captions. Suggest that families help and encourage them with their writing – from apparent scribble with the youngest children, to whole sentences from the more confident writers.

Support and Extension
Thinking about behaviour and keeping the diary are more important in this activity than the actual writing process. More experienced writers can have larger sheets and be encouraged to write in greater detail.

Further Ideas
● Keep a whole-group diary to record kind and thoughtful behaviour. Try to ensure that all the children (and adults) make a contribution during the week.
● Create a 'good behaviour tree' by giving the children a leaf to add whenever they are 'caught' being good.

DRAMA IDEAS

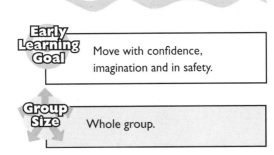

Physical development

Early Learning Goal

Move with confidence, imagination and in safety.

Group Size

Whole group.

Support and Extension

Work with mixed groups so that the confident actors can support the more reluctant ones. Be aware that some children who appear quiet can sometimes enjoy taking a role.

Further Ideas

● Invite Muslim adults to talk to the children about their experiences of fasting.

● Use drama activities to help the children to imagine the feelings of people in other situations such as weddings.

CALLING ALL ACTORS!

What you need

'Eid is here!' photocopiable sheet on page 42; props, such as a table set for dinner and a doll (optional).

Preparation

Arrange the room so that the children can work in designated areas.

What to do

● Read the first half of the story that tells of the family fasting and how they break their fast ready for Eid. Discuss the reasons why Muslims choose to fast with the children. Explain that fasting takes place from dawn to dusk each day for a lunar month. It is broken by eating something sweet, such as dates or fruit in syrup.

● Divide the children into small groups.

● Ask each group to examine the role of a particular character from the story and to imagine how fasting makes a difference to their day.

● Invite the children to act out the following scenes that relate to the characters in the story. Use props if appropriate and ensure that all of the children are included in roles, such as school friends, colleagues or shoppers.

Dad: he looks forward to the period of fasting each year. During the day he finds a quiet space to pray.

Nusrat: her parents have agreed that she can fast. She is thrilled, as she feels she is being treated like an adult. The school has agreed but would like her to drink a little water during the day. At lunchtime the Muslim children can go to a quiet room.

Amjad: although he is too young to fast, he gets accidentally woken up early because the rest of the family want breakfast before dawn. Mum gives him a snack when he gets home from school but he has to wait longer for dinner. He does not really understand why Mum and Dad are more tired than normal. He knows that there will be a celebration at the end and cannot wait for that to happen.

Mum with Omar at home:
she fasts every day but feeds her pre-school child. She does get tired – especially as toddlers are full of energy. She prepares a sugary snack each day for everyone to break their fast.

● Watch each group in turn.

● Involve all of the children in acting the last part of the story with the family having its evening meal together.

(Two weeks before Ramadan, Muslims get ready for the fast by remembering all of the things that they have done wrong and praying to God (Allah) to forgive their sins. This is a story that could be told around this time.)

King Hakim had a beautiful big garden. A poor widow had a little garden next to it, where she grew vegetables. One day the king thought, 'Pity about that vegetable garden! It spoils the view'. He sent a servant to the widow to tell her that he wanted to buy her garden. But the widow said, 'If I can't grow food to eat, I will die'. The servant told King Hakim. He laughed. 'Offer her more money!' The servant came back with a donkey carrying a chest of gold. He told the widow, 'All this is yours if you will sell your garden'. The woman was upset. 'My husband loved this garden. Now God has given it to me. I won't sell it for all the king's gold.' The king was angry. 'Dig up the vegetables and throw her out,' he shouted. The poor widow was crying. She thought, 'I'll find the judge. He'll know what to do'. When the judge came, King Hakim said, 'This woman wouldn't take the gold I offered so we have taken her garden away from her'. The judge knew the king had done wrong and went off to think about what to do.

Next day, everyone met again. The judge had brought a donkey and some sacks. 'Can I have some soil from your garden?' he asked the king. 'Certainly,' said the king, though he was puzzled. His men went to take soil from the widow's garden. 'No,' said the judge, pointing to one of King Hakim's beautiful flowerbeds. 'I want some of that.' The gardeners piled sacks and sacks on to the donkey's back until it couldn't move. The king could bear it no longer. 'Judge, you are a wise man. Why do you want more soil than the donkey can carry?' The judge said, 'Taking the widow's garden was wrong. When we die, we will all meet God, carrying our sins with us. If you keep the widow's garden, you will have more sins than you can carry, just like my donkey with all that soil on his back. You will never get through the gate to Heaven'. Straight away King Hakim was sorry for what he had done. 'May God forgive me!' he cried. He gave the garden back to the widow and ordered his gardeners to plant it with vegetables again. He gave the widow a chest of gold as well, and begged her to forgive him.

Barbara Moore

Mohammed and the old lady

(This is a type of traditional story that would be told during Ramadan. It is presented here as a rhyme.)

Mohammed (peace be with him)
Lived many years ago;
He tried to be a good, kind man –
That's sometimes hard, you know.

There was a cross old lady,
He passed her house each day;
She swept dirt on Mohammed's head
As he went upon his way.

One day, Mohammed passed her house,
No dirt fell on his head;
'Where can that cross old lady be?'
He asked – she was in bed.

She wasn't very well at all,
Mohammed learned that day;
So off he went for food and drink
To take round straight away.

He nursed that cross old lady,
And every night he'd pray
That God would make her better,
As he cared for her each day.

At long last she was well again;
She got up from her bed.
'God bless you, good Mohammed,'
That cross old lady said.

And so from that day onward
That lady changed her ways,
And, like Mohammed, she was good
And kind for all her days.

Barbara Moore

Ramadan is over!

Five pretty Eid cards
Standing in a row,
To wish us luck and happiness
Wherever we may go.

Four shiny paper chains
To make the room look bright;
Gold and red and silver, too,
Ready for Eid night.

Three new suits all hanging up,
The best we've ever had –
One for me and one for Mum,
And the biggest one for Dad.

Two small hands with patterns
That my auntie made last night,
Golden brown and beautiful –
She painted them just right!

One new moon is shining,
Silvery and clear;
Ramadan is over,
And Eid at last is here!

Barbara Moore

RAMADAN
STORY CARDS

● Cut along the dotted lines as indicated to create six story cards.

RAMADAN GAMEBOARD

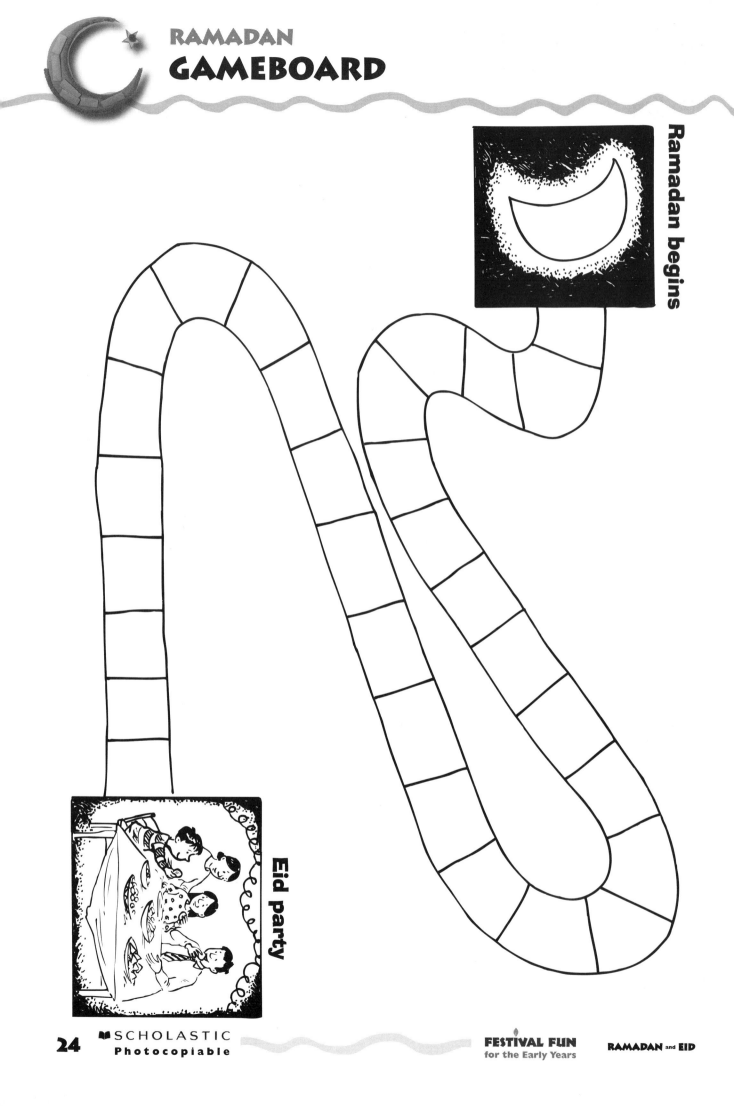

Ramadan begins

Eid party

FESTIVAL FUN
for the Early Years

RAMADAN and EID

● Cut along the lines indicated.

Fold and glue here

Fold and glue here

Monday	Tuesday
Wednesday	**Thursday**
Friday	**Saturday**
Sunday	My Ramadan diary by _____

EID
BACKGROUND INFORMATION AND PLANNING

Dates

● Muslims use a lunar calendar for their observances, with a new month starting with the appearance of the crescent moon. The festival date, therefore, appears to move but it is always at the end of the ninth month – Ramadan.

● Preparations for Eid start during the last week of Ramadan, during which the majority of people have been fasting from sunrise to sunset.

● The three-day-long celebrations are very much a family occasion.

Religious beliefs

● Muslims all over the world follow the teachings of the Qur'an. Muslims are still taught to recite the Qur'an in Arabic although it has now been translated into more than 40 languages.

● Eid-ul-Fitr is one of the two major Islamic festivals (the other is Eid-ul-Adha which ends the period of Hajj when Muslims try to visit the holy city of Makkah). The name comes from the Arabic – 'Eid', happiness and festivity, with 'Fitr' – breaking fasts.

● During the previous month of Ramadan, Muslims fast from dawn to dusk. They consider what it must be like to be poor and needy. During Eid they thank God for all the good that they have in their lives.

● Eid is also a time to ask for God's mercy and help to live in the ways taught in the Qur'an.

● The central principles of Islam can be found in the Five Pillars of Islam. Muslims accept the declaration of faith (Shahadah), which states that there is only one God, Allah, and that Mohammed is the messenger of God. Mohammed was a teacher who demonstrated the way that Muslims should live. Muslims pray five times a day (Salah). They also have a duty to give to the poor and needy (Zakah). Another Pillar of Islam is fasting (Sawm) during the month of Ramadan and culminating in the festival of Eid-ul-Fitr. The final Pillar is the pilgrimage to Makkah (Hajj). Muslims try to do this at least once during their lifetime.

Customs and traditions

● Muslims all around the world celebrate Eid. There are, however, local variations in the ways in which the festival is celebrated. In some areas of the world there might be street parades, parties, music and decorations, whereas in other places celebrations might be concentrated in the home and the Mosque.

● During Eid relatives are visited and food is shared. Many people have new clothes. Gifts are given which often consist of money, sweets or dried fruits.

● Greeting cards are exchanged between friends. These will be decorated with patterns rather than pictures and they are frequently in blue and green, representing heaven and earth. It should be remembered that Arabic is written from right to left, and cards open accordingly.

EID
BACKGROUND INFORMATION AND PLANNING

● In many countries, for example, India and Pakistan, women and girls decorate the palm of their hands with mehndi patterns. This traditional decoration might also be used by Hindu and Sikh women at other celebrations, such as weddings. The patterns are made with a henna (mehndi) paste and last from one to four weeks.

Celebrations

● Eid is a time of great joy following Ramadan. Most forms of celebration are permitted but there will be no alcohol or gambling.

● The festival begins with the sighting of the new moon. Many people wait at the Mosque until they see it or until a message arrives from an area of the world where it is less cloudy.

● The day starts with bathing followed by special prayers at the Mosque. Congregations are usually large with the prayers being lead by the 'Imam'. The Imam is a member of the community who is knowledgeable about the Qur'an. Some women might prefer to pray at home or in a separate part of the Mosque. When leaving, worshippers will greet each other with 'Eid Mubarak' (Happy Eid).

● Much of the day is spent visiting relatives and exchanging gifts. The family meal usually takes place around midday. It is a particularly joyful time being the first daytime meal together for a month. Families try to provide the best meal that they can afford.

● The day ends in prayer – one of the five times a day that Muslims generally pray.

● The celebrations generally continue for three days in predominantly Muslim countries.

Things to remember

● When organising any activity which includes food or drink, it is important to check first with families or carers for any food allergies or dietary requirements of the children.

● Owing to certain customs, some of the children will be reluctant to take part in anything involving music and singing, or have their photographs taken. It is important to talk to families about their own traditions and not to make assumptions.

● When acting stories, the character of the Prophet Mohammed should not be portrayed.

Using the poster

● Muslims live by strict dietary laws that relate to conditions in the seventh century. Pork is not allowed but other meat is, if it is 'halal' (the animal being killed according to Muslim tradition). Alcohol is forbidden. Many Muslims also avoid foods containing lard, gelatine or blood products.

● Families enjoy special foods at Eid, but the food eaten depends on the traditions of the local area. Look at the people attending the meal in the poster. Notice the different generations. On what other occasions might families gather together in a similar way?

Happy Eid

HAPPY Eid

Eid Mubarak

CROSS-CURRICULAR IDEAS

Personal, social and emotional development

WAIT FOR EID!

What you need
Familiar object to pass around the circle, such as a favourite soft toy or a large shell.

What to do
● Ask the children to sit in a circle.
● Explain that you are going to have a circle-time discussion. Make group decisions about acceptable behaviour, for example, let people know you are listening by being still, only talk when you have the object, all comments should be positive and so on.
● Remind the children that, during Ramadan, Muslim children look forward to Eid. Talk to them about an event that you look forward to and explain any hopes and fears, such as seeing a friend again or forgetting something.
● Ask the children to take turns to talk about an event that they anticipate. Be sensitive to the needs of individual children.

> **Early Learning Goal**
> Have a developing awareness of their own needs, views and feelings and be sensitive to the needs, views and feelings of others.

> **Talk About**
> Discuss the ways in which Muslim families wait for Eid. Talk about waiting for the new moon. Sometimes cloud cover makes it difficult to see, so families wait for telephone calls from relatives elsewhere to know when Eid starts.

DRESS FOR THE PARTY!

What you need
Hand-washing facilities; soap; area to hang clothes; clothes hangers, spare clothes and labels for children who are unable to provide their own.

Preparation
Inform parents and carers of the party and ask them to provide a change of clothes and a named hanger, explaining that the children will be playing games and eating party food. This activity is linked to 'Eid party list' on page 31, 'Yummy party sandwiches!' on page 37 and 'It's party time!' on page 40.

What to do
● Ask the children to prepare for the Eid party. Remind them that it is always important to wash their hands before eating.
● Invite the children to hang up their clothes to prevent creasing.
● Encourage the children to help each other with clothes fastenings. Use appropriate vocabulary, such as 'stretchy', 'elastic' and 'buckle'.
● Ask the children to turn the clothes they take off the right way round and fold or hang them.
● Wear the clothes to the party and have a good time!

> **Early Learning Goal**
> Dress and undress independently and manage their own personal hygiene.

> **Talk About**
> Muslim children will often have new clothes for Eid. The style will depend on the cultural background of the families concerned.

> **Further Ideas**
> ● Encourage the children to talk about their own experiences of celebrations.
> ● Use artefacts familiar to Muslim children in the role-play area. Include books written in Arabic and other relevant languages.

Communication, language and literacy

EID PARTY LIST

What you need
Whiteboards or large sheets of paper; writing materials.

Preparation
Make sure that the children's families are informed of the party well in advance. This activity is linked to 'Dress for the party!' on page 30, 'Yummy party sandwiches!' on page 37 and 'It's party time!' on page 40.

What to do
- Ask the children to help you make plans for the party.
- Discuss the areas to consider. Work with the children to write a 'to do' list. Encourage the children to suggest things, such as games to play, who to invite, clearing up, food and drink, and making decorations.
- Let small groups of children each choose one of these areas and ask them to prepare a list for this.
- Support the more experienced children to write a 'to do' list of their own. This might include bringing in food from home and a change of clothes. Ask the children to share this list with their families.
- Refer to the lists as the preparations take place and delete each item as it is completed.

Early Learning Goal Attempt writing for different purposes, using features of different forms such as lists, stories and instructions.

Talk About Discuss the reasons for celebrating at this time. Remind the group that Eid follows Ramadan and that it is a happy religious and family occasion.

WHICH LANGUAGE?

What you need
Copy of 'Many languages!' photocopiable sheet on page 45 for each child; examples of local community languages; writing materials.

What to do
- Demonstrate how to write 'Eid Mubarak' (Happy Eid) in English. Emphasise the correct place to start on the page and how to move from left to right.
- Show the children the writing of 'Eid Mubarak' in different languages on the photocopiable sheet.
- Encourage the children to look closely at the different writing styles – do they recognise any of the letters?
- Ask the group to write 'Eid Mubarak' both in English and a different language. This can be by following the line, tracing or copying, according to the children's level of development.

Early Learning Goal Know that print carries meaning and, in English, is read from left to right and top to bottom.

Talk About Ask the children if they know of anyone who can read different languages. Explain that the Qur'an is written in Arabic. Many adult Muslims learn to read the Qur'an in Arabic but also speak the language of their own local community and English.

Further Ideas
- Prepare a display of relevant books and provide opportunities for the children to discuss them.
- Play a game where each child repeats a sentence adding on a new word or phrase each time, for example, 'We made cards', 'We made cards and food', 'We made cards and food and a mobile'.

CROSS-CURRICULAR IDEAS

Mathematical development

SYMMETRY! SYMMETRY!

Early Learning Goal
Use everyday words to describe position.

Talk About
Explain to the children that much of Islamic decoration is symmetrical. Look for similarities in Islamic art from different parts of the world.

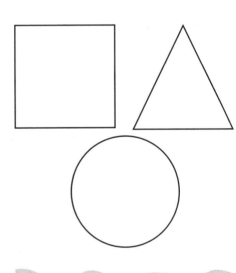

What you need
Examples of symmetrical shapes cut out of paper; rulers or pieces of string; vocabulary cards; variety of symmetrical objects from around the setting; display area and materials, such as backing paper or fabric; camera (optional – a digital camera is preferable since it gives an immediate result).

What to do
● Show the children examples of symmetry using paper. Demonstrate how the symmetrical paper shapes can be folded with the sides matching exactly. Let the children experiment.
● Choose some common objects from around the setting, such as a book, toy or box. Show the symmetry in them. Use a ruler or piece of string to show the axis of symmetry.
● Ask the children to identify objects that they believe to be symmetrical. Talk about the way in which both sides have similar shapes. Use appropriate vocabulary, such as 'same', 'different', 'right', 'left', 'top', 'bottom' and 'middle'.
● Make a collection of the smaller objects and arrange them in a display with the vocabulary cards. Talk to the children about why they chose the objects.
● Take photographs of the larger objects and add these to the display. Encourage the children to take the pictures by themselves if possible.

MEHNDI FUN

Early Learning Goal
Talk about, recognise and recreate simple patterns.

Talk About
Explain that mehndi patterns are cultural and are also used during celebrations within Hinduism and Sikhism. These patterns remain for several weeks so it is not advisable to make these on the children's hands.

Further Ideas
● Use the hands to create a decorative border. Arrange them in a repetitive pattern, for example, two left, two right and so on.

What you need
Copy of 'Mehndi patterns' photocopiable sheet on page 46 for each child; drawing paper in appropriate skin tones; scissors; colouring and drawing materials.

What to do
● Discuss the mehndi patterns on the photocopiable sheet. Explain that women and girls often decorate their hands during the Eid celebrations.
● Ask the children to draw around their own or a partner's hands, assisting as required.
● Cut out the paper hands for the children.
● Ask the children to work in pairs to decorate both right and left paper hands. Explain that the actual patterns would probably be a shade of brown. They can either keep with tradition or choose their own colours.
● Remind the group to refer to and copy the sample patterns on the photocopiable sheet.

EID
CROSS-CURRICULAR IDEAS

SPECIAL MESSAGES

What you need
Paper; writing materials; pretend or real telephone; computer.

What to do
● Explain that towards the end of Ramadan, when the new moon is first seen, Muslims communicate with each other to spread the word that the Eid festival can begin.
● Consider the different ways that messages can be transmitted. List all of the children's suggestions.
● Support the children in sending messages about Eid and the new moon in a wide variety of ways, including writing and delivering a letter, making a telephone call and sending an email. These could be sent 'for real' or in a role-play situation.
● Discuss the most suitable method for convenience, speed and accuracy.

Early Learning Goal Find out about and identify the uses of everyday technology and use information and communication technology and programmable toys to support their learning.

Talk About Discuss how it feels to receive a message. Explain that there are times when Muslims are unable to see the new moon because of cloud cover. It is therefore important for them to receive messages from elsewhere.

CELEBRATIONS

What you need
Two large sheets of paper; two large hoops; small pieces of cards; writing and drawing materials.

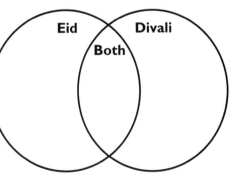

What to do
● On one sheet of paper, work with the children to list the various ways to celebrate Eid, including decorating your home, visiting friends and relatives, preparing special food, visiting the Mosque, sending cards, going to parties and so on.
● Take a new sheet of paper to compile a second list of various ways to celebrate a festival from a different faith, such as Christmas, Pesach or Divali.
● Match the two lists and discuss their similarities and differences.
● Write all of the suggestions on small pieces of card and ask the children to illustrate them.
● Place the two hoops on the floor and overlap them. Label the three sections as 'Eid', 'Both' and the name of the other festival.
● Discuss each card with the children and decide where it should be placed in the hoops.

Early Learning Goal Begin to know about their own cultures and beliefs and those of other people.

Talk About Discuss the common elements found in celebrations. Many of these may also be seen in smaller celebrations, such as birthdays and weddings. Talk about why some elements only appear once, for example, the Christmas tree relates to a specific festival.

Further Ideas
● Give the children the opportunity to describe celebrations within their own families.
● Taste foods that are eaten in celebrations for different cultures, for example, Jamaican Easter Bun, Indian sweets at Divali and so on. Remember to check first with families for any food allergies or dietary requirements.
● Make a book to record the preparations for Eid.
● Talk to Muslims about their experiences of Eid.

CROSS-CURRICULAR IDEAS

Physical development

Talk About
Explain that most Islamic decoration is shaped on geometric patterns. During Ramadan and Eid, the moon is particularly significant as Eid starts at the time of the sighting of the new moon. Discuss the shape of the moon and stars.

Early Learning Goal
Handle tools, objects, construction and malleable materials safely and with increasing control.

Talk About
Discuss other symbols that are important to the children or members of their families, such as the symbol of a club or another religious symbol.

Further Ideas
● Use vocabulary in drama to express feelings of anticipation and excitement, either individually or in a group.
● Encourage the children to try foods that are new to them. Explain that they can be both healthy and enjoyable.

GREAT SHAPES!

What you need
Wide variety of PE and play equipment, for example, ropes, hoops, benches, tricycle, chalk and beanbags.

What to do
● Set out the area (preferably outdoors) as an obstacle course with a difference. Try to make each activity based on a geometric shape. For example:
– arrange benches as a triangle or rectangle, and ask the children to move along each side in a different way
– hop or jump between hoops set out in a symmetrical pattern
– cycle slowly along a crescent, moon-shaped chalk track
– throw a beanbag to each point of a star marked on the ground
– walk heel-to-toe along the sides of a chalk square.
● When the tasks are completed, involve the children in returning the equipment to the correct places.

MODEL MOON

What you need
Large mixing bowl; water; salt; food colouring; flour; perfume (optional); protected surface or boards; crescent moon-shaped templates or cutters; modelling knife (adult use only); modelling tools, symmetrical shapes to press into the dough; oven (optional); yellow paint.

What to do
● Mix the dough in sufficient quantity for the number of children in the group, in the proportion of 1 cup water, 1 cup salt, a little food colouring and 2 cups flour. Mix them in the above order. A little perfume could also be added. Knead the dough thoroughly.
● Ask the children to make their piece of dough into a roughly shaped thick circle, rectangle or square.
● Give the children the crescent moon-shaped templates or cutters. Assist them to cut the shape halfway through the middle of their dough. Ask an adult to do this with the modelling knife if the children are using templates.
● Let the children flatten the surrounding area to give a raised shape plaque and tidy the edges to remake the square, circle or rectangle.
● Make a patterned symmetrical border for the plaque, using fingers, modelling tools or different shapes.
● Dry the dough slowly in the oven at a low temperature.
● When dry and cool, invite the children to paint the moon yellow.

EID
CROSS-CURRICULAR IDEAS

Creative development

<table>
<tr><td>**Early Learning Goal**</td><td>Explore colour, texture, shape, form and space in two or three dimensions.</td></tr>
</table>

Talk About | Explain the way in which Muslim families wait for the new moon to begin their Eid celebrations.

HAPPY EID!

What you need
'Make a card' photocopiable sheet on page 47; dark blue sheets of A4 paper and yellow paper for each child; glue; sticky tape; thread; child scissors; silver or gold pens.

Preparation
Enlarge and copy the 'Make a card' photocopiable sheet on page 47 on to the blue paper, so that the card will be a folded piece of A4 with the circle in the middle of the front page. Enlarge and copy on to yellow paper the moon shape and 'Eid Mubarak'.

What to do
● Give each child a 'card' and show them how to fold it in half.
● Demonstrate how to cut out the circle, keeping the card in tact, and supervise the children while they work.
● Assist the children as they cut out their yellow moon shape.
● Use sticky tape to attach thread to the moon and to the inside of the front of the card, so that the moon hangs in the middle of the cut-out circle.
● Let the children cut out their 'Eid Mubarak' and glue it on to the front. Ask them to write their names on the inside at the bottom of the card, using gold or silver pens.

MOON POEM

What you need
Variety of pictures and poems about the moon; large sheets of paper; pens.

What to do
● Show the pictures of the moon to the group and ask the children to describe the moon's appearance.
● Make a list of appropriate words and phrases together, for example, 'bumpy', 'watery', 'bright' and 'cheerful'.
● Read the poems, suggesting that the children close their eyes to picture the moon.
● Choose one poem to add a verse to. Re-read it and clap to find the rhythm of the lines.
● Work with the children to write the new verse for the poem, using words and phrases from the previously listed vocabulary.

Early Learning Goal | Recognise and explore how sounds can be changed, sing simple songs from memory, recognise repeated sounds and sound patterns and match movements to music.

Talk About | Discuss the way in which the moon can affect how people feel and how valuable it can be at night, for example, allowing people to see, helping with directions and indicating the months and seasons.

Further Ideas | ● Ask the children to write a poem by themselves about the excitement of seeing the moon so that the Eid celebrations can begin.
● Design a poster for the Eid celebrations. Use the 'Many languages!' photocopiable sheet on page 45, either cutting out or copying the words as a starting point.

EID
CRAFT AND GIFT IDEAS

Creative development

BOX OF DELIGHTS

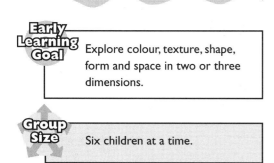

Explore colour, texture, shape, form and space in two or three dimensions.

Early Learning Goal

Group Size

Six children at a time.

What you need
Two squares of stiff paper (27cm×27cm) for each child; green ribbon; sticky tape; glue; decorative materials, such as felt-tipped pens or glitter pens; commercial or homemade sweets; child scissors.

Preparation
Fold each square into three, both vertically and horizontally, to give nine small squares to make a small box. Open the paper and mark the squares to be cut by the children (see illustration). Cut the ribbon in strips, long enough to go round the box twice and tie with a bow. Make up a box to use for demonstration purposes. Check with the children's families for any food allergies or dietary requirements.

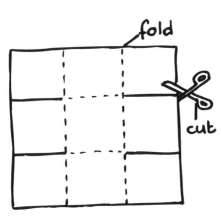

Support and Extension

Less experienced children will need support with cutting and folding accurately. They could also replace the lid with a handle made from ribbon. Encourage older children to make their decorations symmetrical.

What to do
● Tell the children that they are going to make a 'box of delights' to take home. Show them the sample box and the sweets.
● Give each child a square and ask them to cut in the places indicated. The children should be supervised while cutting.
● Ask the children to follow your demonstration as you fold up the sides of the square to form a box. Encourage them to make very definite and precise folds.
● Support the children to fix the sides in place.
● Make the lid with the second square of paper in the same way, letting the children decorate the squares in the middle of each side. Use the shape of the moon as the basis for their decorations.
● Ensure that the decorated squares are on the outside as the children fold and stick down the sides.
● Fill the box with sweets. These can be made by the children on a separate occasion or commercially produced.
● Cover the box with the lid and stick the ribbon in place. Help the children to stick one piece around the lid and a longer piece to the base. Tie this piece on top in a bow.
● Take the box home during the Eid celebrations.

Further Ideas

● Make stuffed dates with the children to fill the boxes – see 'Stuffed dates' activity on page 15.
● Create a bookmark for a family member or friend. Write the name of the recipient in large, clear writing along the length of the bookmark. Decorate using designs inspired by examples of Islamic art. Show the children examples of Islamic calligraphy, which is a popular art form.

EID
COOKERY IDEAS

Mathematical development

YUMMY PARTY SANDWICHES!

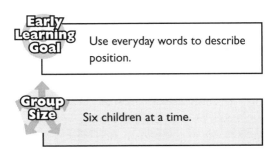

Early Learning Goal
Use everyday words to describe position.

Group Size
Six children at a time.

What you need
Clean table covering; cookery aprons; spreading knives; star- and moon-shaped cutters; sharp knife (adult use only); serving plates; variety of different breads (supermarkets and specialist shops provide a wide selection of breads, such as pitta, Jamaican hardo and ciabatta); margarine; equipment to prepare fillings, including chopping board and grater (adult use only); vegetarian fillings (most Muslim children will eat meat but only if it is specially prepared halal meat); hand-washing facilities; silver foil.

Preparation
Find out from the children's families if they have any food allergies or dietary requirements. Involve small groups of children in the preparation of the ingredients and setting out the area, as long as it is safe to do so. Ensure that the area is clean and all hands are washed. Prepare the various fillings. This activity is linked to 'Dress for the party!' on page 30, 'Eid party list' on page 31 and 'It's party time!' on page 40.

What to do
● Tell the children that they are going to prepare some sandwiches that will be appropriate for the Eid celebrations. Explain why the sandwiches will be shaped like the moon and stars, and why the fillings will be vegetarian. Point out that the breads are from around the world because Eid is celebrated globally.
● Discuss the need for cleanliness when dealing with food.
● Use star and moon cutters to cut the bread. Discuss the placement of the cutters on the bread so as to avoid waste. Use vocabulary such as 'next to', 'close' and 'near'.
● Encourage the children to make up the sandwiches with an appropriate amount of filling.

Support and Extension
Some children may need assistance when using spreading knives to spread the fillings on to the bread. The use of vocabulary can be differentiated according to the development of each child. Some of them might need encouragement to try types of bread that are new to them.

Further Ideas
● Make other food that is suitable for an Eid party, such as biscuits, cakes and jellies. Pay particular attention to specific dietary needs, for example, some Muslim children do not eat jelly containing gelatine.
● Discuss the number of sandwiches needed for the size of the group.
● Set out the tables for the whole group to share the food. Ensure that there is one place set for each child. This can be used as an opportunity to reinforce number concepts.

● Arrange the completed sandwiches on serving plates. Talk about the arrangement and positioning of the sandwiches. Are they in front, beside, under or on top? Encourage the children to take care with the presentation.
● Cover the sandwiches with silver foil to keep them fresh. Share them out later with the whole group.
● Include the children in the tidying and cleaning – taking particular care with knives.

EID
DISPLAY IDEAS

Knowledge and understanding of the world

Early Learning Goal
Begin to know about their own cultures and beliefs and those of other people.

Group Size
Small groups.

Support and Extension
Some children might require support to provide paintings of an appropriate size. Extend this activity by encouraging the children to write 'Happy Eid' in the speech bubbles.

Further Ideas
● Make a display to record the group's Eid activities. Include comments from children and adults, photographs (if parental consent has been given) and any items made by the children.
● Display symmetrical patterns made by the children, together with examples of mehndi patterns.

EID MUBARAK

What you need
'Many languages!' photocopiable sheet on page 45, plus other examples of 'Happy Eid' written in languages spoken by the families of children in the group; display board; backing paper; child scissors; glue; painting paper; paints and crayons, including skin, hair and eye colours appropriate for the children in the group; paintbrushes; unbreakable mirror; painting aprons; white paper; brightly coloured paper.

Preparation
Remember to obtain parental consent for this activity from Muslim parents. Prepare the painting area and set out the paper for the self-portraits. Create a display board. Cut out lettering for the title 'Happy Eid' and 'Eid Mubarak' using brightly coloured paper. Make copies of 'Happy Eid' in different languages including those from the photocopiable sheet. Draw speech bubbles on to white paper.

What to do
● Show the children the display board and explain that it is for their self-portraits.
● Use the mirror and describe your own features to the children. Talk about hair, eyes and skin. Explain that the children will need to mix paint or use a crayon to find their nearest skin colour. Tell them that the paper should not be left untouched, as it is very rare to have white skin.
● Help the children to put on their painting aprons and ask them to paint their portraits.
● In some cases, skin colour will be easier to match with crayon. If so, arrange for the children to complete this part of the portrait when the painted sections are dry.
● Write the children's names on the paintings and leave them to dry.
● When dry, cut out the paintings and arrange them on the display board.
● Explain that you would like to record what the children are saying by using speech bubbles. Show the children the different versions of 'Happy Eid' on the photocopiable sheet. Ask them if they have any preferences for languages. Do they know anyone who speaks one of the languages shown?
● Assist the children to cut out their chosen version of 'Happy Eid' and glue it into a paper speech bubble. Position them next to the self-portraits. Complete the display by adding the title 'Happy Eid' and 'Eid Mubarak'.

EID
ROLE-PLAY IDEAS

Personal, social and emotional development

Early Learning Goal
Work as part of a group or class, taking turns and sharing fairly, understanding that there needs to be agreed values and codes of behaviour for groups of people, including adults and children, to work together harmoniously.

Group Size
All of the children working in pairs.

Support and Extension
Allocate cleaning roles according to the ability of the children. When pairing the children, put confident children with those requiring support. An adult should support the children performing the washing tasks and make sure that they are not walking on slippery floors.

Further Ideas
● Extend the cleaning and decorating to other areas of the setting.

● Encourage the children to incorporate their own ideas into the decorations. Remind them that they need to be appropriate for this Muslim festival.

● Invite adults to see the prepared area. Encourage the children to be proud of their achievements as a group.

LET'S GET READY!

What you need
Washing and cleaning materials, including floor brush and pan, dusters, soap and water; dolls and dolls' clothes and equipment; paper; pen; Eid decorations; Blu-Tack; sticky tape.

Preparation
Set up the role-play area for the children to clean, tidy and decorate. It should include somewhere where the children can wash the dolls' clothes and the dolls' equipment. Write a list of cleaning activities for the children to choose from.

What to do
● Explain that, in preparing for Eid, most Muslim families will clean their homes and decorate them. You would like the children to do the same in the role-play area. Ask the children to choose which cleaning activity they would like to do from your list. These might include:
– sweeping the floor
– dusting
– washing the dolls' clothes and equipment
– tidying up.

● Put the children into pairs. As they work, talk to them about the activity. Discuss the importance of cleanliness and hygiene.

● When everywhere is clean, tidy and dry, the children can begin to decorate for the festival celebrations. If possible, use the pieces made in previous activities, including:
– 'Star and moon mobile' (see page 13)
– 'Black and white art' (see page 13)
– 'Picture the moon!' (see page 14)
– 'Model moon' (see page 34)
– 'Happy Eid!' (see page 35).

● Talk to the children about the placing of decorations. Assist them with positioning in high places.

● Dress the dolls in their best clothes.

● Let the children enjoy playing in the role-play area in small groups – taking care to leave it clean and tidy.

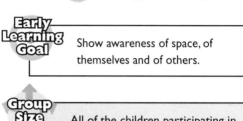

Physical development

IT'S PARTY TIME!

What you need
Space to hold a party; tables; chairs or benches; placemats; paper or plastic plates; plastic glasses; prizes for games; party food and drinks; decorations.

Preparation
Arrange for additional adult assistance for this activity. Inform families about the party and ask them to send a change of clothes for the children. Acquire food and suitable drinks (families are often willing to contribute) and check with parents or carers for any food allergies or dietary requirements. Decorate the room. This activity is linked to 'Dress for the party!' on page 30, 'Eid party list' on page 31 and 'Yummy party sandwiches!' on page 37.

What to do
● Explain to the children that you need to prepare for a party and you would like their assistance and suggestions.
● Discuss the arrangement of the room, for example, how the tables should be placed and whether there will be enough chairs for everyone.
● Work with small groups of children to organise the furniture and set the table. As you do so, talk about the need for such things as space between the tables so that the adults can give the children their party food and drinks.
● Talk about the games area. Is there enough space for the whole group to play together?
● During the party, play games that involve using the whole of the space available. Games where the children need to freeze or jump into a hoop when they hear a specified word will lend themselves to this activity.

● Ask the children to make good use of the space available. At the same time, they need to be aware of the nearness of other children. Remind them that they should not push, shove or knock into others when playing.
● Give prizes to the children who win the games, while emphasising the fun of taking part.
● Enjoy the party!

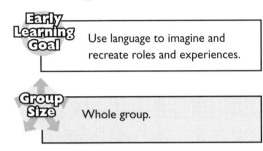

EID

DRAMA IDEAS

Communication, language and literacy

A FAMILY AT EID

Early Learning Goal
Use language to imagine and recreate roles and experiences.

Group Size
Whole group.

What you need
'Eid is here' photocopiable sheet on page 42; 'Let's celebrate' photocopiable sheet on page 44; props and dressing-up clothes; decorations; pretend sweets and food; 'scenery', including a kitchen area, dinner table and an area to represent the Mosque; drinks and biscuits; homemade cards saying 'Happy Eid' or 'Eid Mubarak'.

Preparation
Prepare the scenery and make the pretend dinner and sweets. If there are Muslim children in the group, choose food that is relevant to their community and culture. Make the cards and decorations.

What to do
● Read the children the story on page 42. Discuss it, explaining any parts they do not fully understand.
● Say that one of the characters in the story has written a poem about Eid. Read 'Let's celebrate!' to the children. Can anyone guess who is 'telling' the poem? (Amjad.)
● Retell 'Eid is here!'. As a character is mentioned, ask all of the group to act that part. Talk about how the characters might feel, for example, when the children go to bed on the eve of Eid they are full of anticipation, and next morning they would be excitedly waking their parents. Use appropriate vocabulary to describe these feelings.
● While asking all of the children to take part, watch for children who appear confident to take on a particular role.
● Ask the children to take specific roles from the story. Perhaps grandparents and a postal worker could be added.
● Retell the story with the children joining in at appropriate times.
● Set a time and date for the performance, and invite an audience of other children or families.
● On the day of the performance, arrange the setting, including an area for the audience.
● Dress the 'actors' and see that they are in their starting positions.
● Welcome the audience. Explain that this is part of the children's celebration of the Muslim religious festival of Eid.
● Retell the story while the children perform.
● Publicly praise all of the children for their efforts. Reward them with drinks and biscuits afterwards.

Support and Extension
Some children might be reluctant to act. If they are really not happy with being part of the group in the story, then encourage them to dress up and welcome the audience at the door. Confident children could have a speaking part.

Further Ideas
● Ask a confident child (or children) to take on the role of Amjad and read out the poem 'Let's celebrate' at the beginning of the play.
● Take photographs (with parental consent) to make a book as a permanent record of the event. Families who were unable to attend could use this to discuss the play with their child.

EID
EID IS HERE!

Nusrat and Amjad were very excited. The sun was going down; soon the new moon would be shining in the sky. They had been waiting for this night during all the weeks of Ramadan. Nusrat was very hungry; she hadn't eaten anything since breakfast, before the sun came up. All she'd had all day was a drink of water at school. Mum had explained that it was important to know how it felt to be hungry, and to remember that some poor people never have enough to eat. Amjad was only six, so he was too young to go all day without food, but Nusrat was nine years old, and for the first time her mum and dad had let her fast for Ramadan, like the grown-ups.

Nusrat was helping her mum to prepare the evening meal, and Amjad was playing with Omar, their little brother. Dad was at the Mosque; as soon as the new moon appeared in the sky, he would come home. Just then, Amjad shouted, 'I can see the moon! Look!'. Nusrat and her mum looked out of the window. The thin silvery moon was shining through a tree. 'Eid Mubarak! Happy Eid!' said Nusrat, and gave her mum a big hug. They heard Dad at the door, and Amjad ran to meet him. He wanted to be the first to say 'Eid Mubarak'. Soon they were all sitting down with a sweet milky drink and some honey cakes. Later they had a proper dinner, with samosas and kebabs. Everything seemed especially tasty!

Next morning was the festival day. Everyone was wearing new clothes. Mum and Nusrat had beautiful mehndi patterns on their hands. They were going to visit their auntie and uncle with sweets and presents. Nusrat and Amjad had made Eid cards at school. 'How lovely!' said Auntie Maryam. Uncle Ali told them they were very clever. When they got home, Mum and Dad and Nusrat got busy making an evening meal for some new friends. Dad had met Ahmed at the Mosque. Ahmed and his family had moved all the way from Africa. Mum and Dad wanted to share their Eid meal with them to make them feel happy and at home.

At last everything was ready, and the guests arrived with sweets and presents. 'Eid Mubarak! Happy Eid!' everyone said, and they all sat down to share a delicious meal together.

Barbara Moore

SCHOLASTIC
Photocopiable

FESTIVAL FUN
for the Early Years

RAMADAN and **EID**

Eid night

Star light, new moon bright,
High up in the sky tonight,
Shining bright, shining clear,
Telling us that Eid is here.

'Eid Mubarak, Eid Mubarak,
Happy Eid!' we say;
Tomorrow we will have a feast,
It's such a happy day.

At school we'll have a party,
With bright new clothes to wear,
And games to play with all our friends,
And lovely food to share.

We always must remember
To thank God as we pray,
For family and clothes and food
He gives us every day.

Barbara Moore

EID RHYMES

Let's celebrate!

It's Eid, it's time to celebrate
With family and friends,
With cards and presents, new clothes too,
As Ramadan now ends.

My family, Nusrat, mum and dad –
All during Ramadan –
Didn't eat from dawn till dusk,
Obeying the Qur'an.

For in our Holy Book it says
That everyone should think,
Of all the people who don't have
Enough to eat and drink.

Omar and I, we didn't fast,
We are too young, they say;
We're growing still; when we grow up
We'll fast, too, every day.

Now Ramadan is over,
We'll have a feast at Eid,
And give some food and money
For people still in need.

Barbara Moore

SCHOLASTIC Photocopiable

FESTIVAL FUN for the Early Years   **RAMADAN and EID**

Urdu	عید مبارک
English	HAPPY EID
Bengali	ঈদ মুবারক
Hindi	ईद मुबारक
Punjabi	ਈਦ ਮੁਬਾਰਕ
Chinese	義(国教節)快樂
Gujarati	શુભ ઈદ

EID
MEHNDI PATTERNS

- Enlarge sheet by 200 per cent.

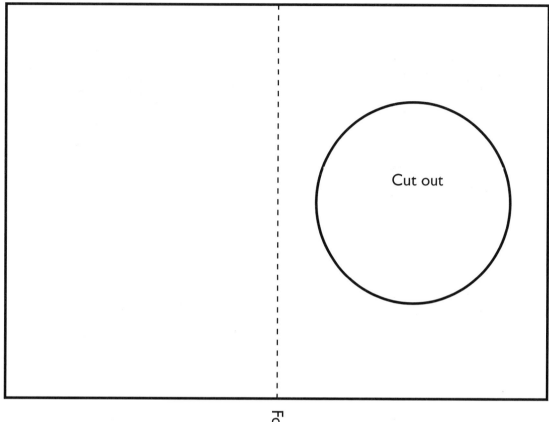

Cut out

Fold

For front of card

Eid Mubarak!

Happy Eid!

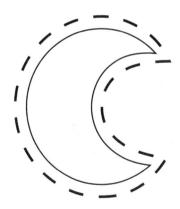

For inside card

Love from

RESOURCES

Books for adults

Mehndi – The Timeless Art of Henna Painting by **Loretta Roome** (Saint Martin's Press)

Mehndi Designs: Traditional Henna Body Art by **Marty Noble** (*Pictorial Archives* series, Dover Publications)

Books for children

Eid Ul-Fitr by **Susheila Stone** (*Celebrations* series, A & C Black)

Samira's Eid by **Nasreen Aktar and Enebor Attard** (Mantra Publishing)

Festivals by **Paul Johnson** (*Copy & Cut* series, A & C Black)

My Muslim Year by **Cath Senker and Shahrukh Husain** (*Year of Religious Festivals* series, Hodder Wayland)

Feasts and Fasting by **Cath Senker** (*Special Ceremonies* series, Hodder Wayland)

Sweet Dates to Eat – A Ramadan and Eid Story by **Jonny Zucker and Jan Barger** (*Festival Time!* series, Frances Lincoln)

The Islamic Year: Surahs, Stories and Celebrations by **Noorah Al-Gailani and Chris Smith** (*Festivals* series, Hawthorn Press)

Muslim Festivals Through the Year by **Anita Ganeri** (*Year of Festivals* series, Franklin Watts)

Ramadan by **Suhaib Hamid Ghazi and Omar Rayyan** (Holiday House)

Ramadan and Id-ul-Fitr by **Mandy Ross** (*Celebrations* series, Heinemann Library)

Id-ul-Fitr by **Mike Hirst** (*Celebrate!* series, Hodder Wayland)

Mohammed and Islam by **Kerena Marchant** (*Great Religious Leaders* series, Hodder Wayland)

Watching the Moon: A Story for Id-ul-Fitr by **Lynne Broadbent and John Logan** (*Time to Remember* series, Religious and Moral Education Press)

Resources

Books, artefacts and posters available from The Festival Shop, 56 Poplar Road, Kings Heath, Birmingham B14 7AG, call 0121-444 0444, email info@festivalshop.co.uk or visit **www.festivalshop.co.uk**

Multicultural resources including religious artefacts and photo packs available from The Parrotfish Company, Laundry Cottage, Church Road, Nacton, Suffolk IP10 OES, call 01473-655007, email enquiries@parrotfish.co.uk or visit **www.parrotfish.co.uk**

Artefacts and other multicultural resources supplied by mail order by Articles of Faith Ltd, Resource House, Kay Street, Bury BL9 6BU, call 0161-763 6232, email ArticlesFaith@cs.com or visit **www.articles offaith.co.uk**

Celebrating Eid Poster available from Mantra Publishing Ltd. A multicultural, multilingual poster that celebrates the diversity of cultures and languages. Visit **www.mantralingua.com**

Ramadan Mubarak video available from Sound Vision. From the *Adam's World* series, Adam learns the importance of Ramadan and fasting in this children's video, which includes songs. Visit **www.islamic goodsdirect.co.uk**

Oriental Arabesque ClipArt available from Sound Vision. A CD-ROM that contains Arabic patterns, letters and ClipArt in colour and black and white, compatible with PC and Mac. Visit **www.islamicgoods direct.co.uk**

Websites

www.bbc.co.uk/religion contains information on a variety of religions as well as views on ethical issues of today, and includes message boards.

http://re-xs.ucsm.ac.uk/ offers resources for teachers, including a news database and information on world religions and ethical issues.

http://islamcity.com contains information and current news regarding various issues of Islamic faith.